Nip, Tap,

Written by Marisa

Illustrated by Raj Patel

Short *Ii* /i/	Consonant *Nn* /n/
it	can
nip	nip
pin	pin
sit	

High-Frequency Words

a	likes	my
I	make	we

1

Nip. Nip.

I make a man.

Tap. Tap.

A bird can sit.

Pin. Pin.

My cat likes it!

We nip, tap, pin!